# Dropping In On...
# SPAIN

## Philip Bader

A Geography Series

THE ROURKE BOOK COMPANY, INC.
VERO BEACH, FLORIDA 32964

**Library of Congress
Cataloging-in-Publication Data**

Bader, Philip, 1969-
   Spain / Philip Bader.
      p.  cm. — (Dropping in on)
   Includes index.
   ISBN 1-55916-282-1
   1. Spain—Description and travel—Juvenile literature.
      [1. Spain—Description and travel.] I. Title. II. Series.

DP43.2 .B33 2000
946 21; aa05 05-09—dc00
                                        00–029073

**Printed in the USA**

# Spain
.......

*Official Name:* Kingdom of Spain

*Area:* 194,897 miles
(504,750 square kilometers)

*Population:* 39,167,744

*Capital:* Madrid (pop. 3,103,000)

*Largest City:* Madrid

*Highest Elevation:*
Pico de Teide (Canary Islands),
12,162 feet (3,707 meters)

*Official Languages:* Castilian Spanish,
Galician, Basque, Catalan

*Major Religion:* Roman Catholic (99%)

*Money:* Peseta

*Form of Government:*
Parliamentary monarchy

*Flag:*

# TABLE OF CONTENTS

# Our Blue Ball—The Earth

The Earth can be divided into two hemispheres. The word hemisphere means "half a ball"—in this case, the ball is the Earth.

The equator is an imaginary line that runs around the middle of the Earth. It separates the Northern Hemisphere from the Southern Hemisphere. North America—where Canada, the United States, and Mexico are located—is in the Northern Hemisphere.

## The Northern Hemisphere

When the North Pole is tilted toward the sun, the sun's most powerful rays strike the northern half of the Earth and less sunshine hits the Southern Hemisphere. That is when people in the Northern Hemisphere enjoy summer. When the

North Pole is tilted away from the sun and the
Southern Hemisphere receives the most sunshine,
the seasons reverse. Then winter comes to the
Northern Hemisphere. Seasons in the Northern
Hemisphere and the Southern Hemisphere are
always opposite.

# Get Ready for Spain

Let's take a trip! Climb into your hot-air balloon, and we'll drop in on a country located at the southern tip of Europe. Spain is bordered to the west by the Atlantic Ocean and Portugal. To the east is the Mediterranean Sea, and to the north the tall Pyrenees Mountains separate Spain from France. The Balearic Islands off the eastern coast and the Canary Islands to the southwest also belong to Spain.

Plains called *mesetas* cover much of Spain's central region. There, the climate is hot and dry. However, many mountain chains line the border regions and extend through parts of central Spain. After Switzerland, Spain has the most mountains in Europe.

Like its landscape, Spain's population differs widely throughout its seventeen independent regions. The Spanish descend from a mixture of Basque, Celtic, Iberian, Greek, Roman, and Visigoth peoples. This rich cultural history is seen today in the many languages and traditions that exist throughout Spain.

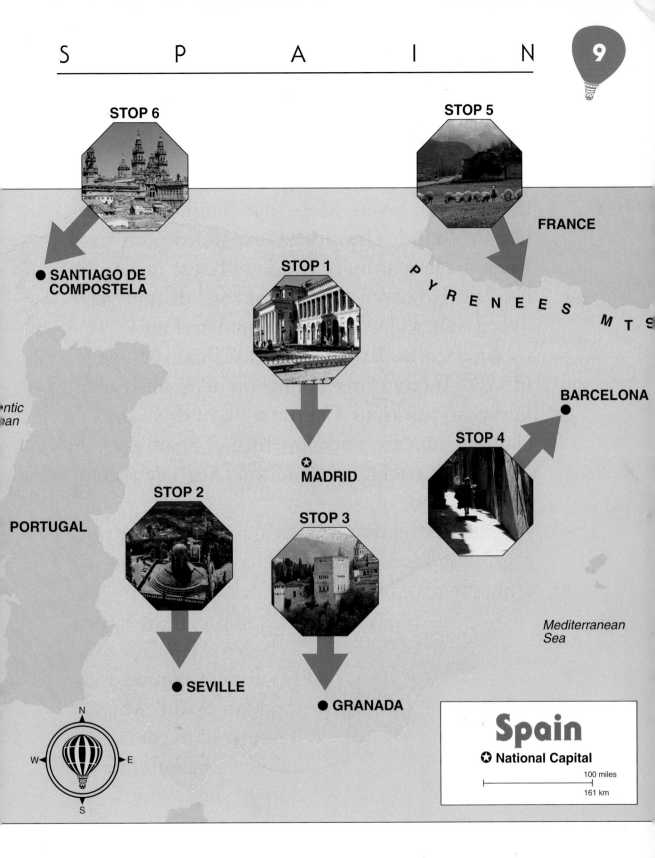

STOP 6

STOP 5

FRANCE

● SANTIAGO DE COMPOSTELA

STOP 1

P Y R E N E E S   M T S

BARCELONA

STOP 4

ntic
ean

MADRID

STOP 2

PORTUGAL

STOP 3

Mediterranean
Sea

● SEVILLE

● GRANADA

N

W ⊕ E

S

**Spain**

✪ National Capital

100 miles
|———————|
161 km

## Stop 1: Madrid

Madrid, the capital, sits on a high plateau in the center of Spain. More than 3 million people live in Madrid. The city has expanded northward, where large apartment buildings house many families. However, Madrid's historic district, just over a mile wide, can be explored on foot.

King Carlos III built Madrid's Prado Museum in 1785. It has a large collection of Spanish and European paintings. On the walls of this world-class museum are works by three of Spain's greatest artists: Francisco Goya, Diego Velásquez, and El Greco.

Outside the city, historical monuments attract tourists and locals who want to escape the busy atmosphere of Madrid. El Escorial Monastery, built 400 years ago, used to be a royal palace. Now, it contains the tombs of Spain's kings. The city of Segovia, an old Roman military outpost, has many well-preserved Roman artifacts.

Atlantic Ocean

1 Madrid

Mediterranean Sea

N
W—E
S

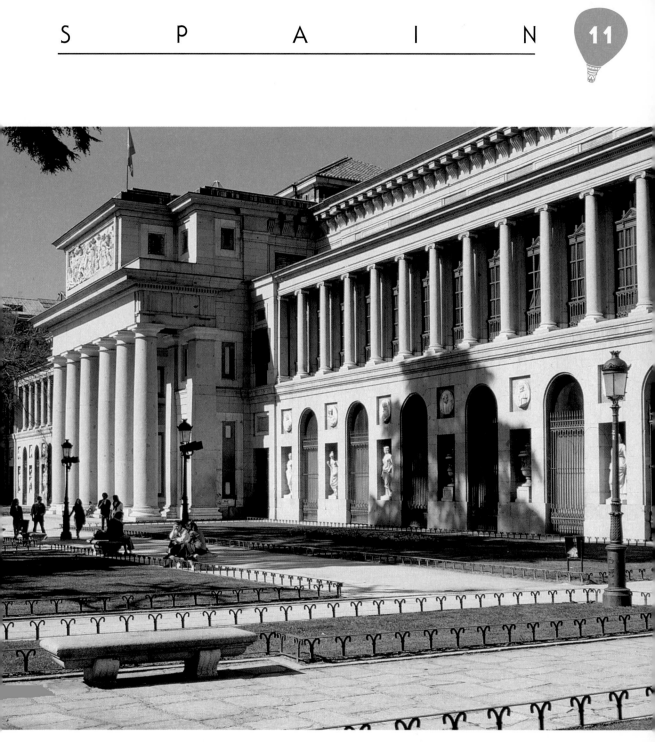

The Prado Museum in Madrid is one of three world-famous museums along the Paseo del Prado.

*Now let's fly **south** to Seville.*

Above: A view of down-
town Seville from the top
of the Cathedral.

Left: A young girl eats
cotton candy during the
Feria de Abril in Seville.

# Stop 2: Seville

Seville, in western Andalusia, is one of the oldest and largest cities in southern Spain. Plazas and waterfront avenues line the banks of the Guadalquivir River that runs through Seville.

Roman armies conquered this region in 205 B.C.E. Later, *Moors* occupied the city. These conquerors built a fortress called the Alcazar and a large *mosque*. Today, a cathedral, the third largest church in the world, covers the original mosque. All that remains of the original building is a courtyard and the Giralda tower, one of the most famous landmarks in Seville.

Each year, Seville celebrates religious and cultural festivals that attract people from all parts of Spain. The *Feria de Abril* (April Fair) includes horse parades, fireworks, dancing, and singing. Another celebration, *Semana Santa* (Holy Week), is one of the most important celebrations of the year.

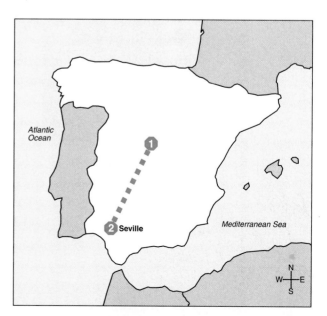

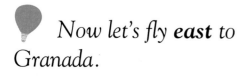

*Now let's fly **east** to Granada.*

# Semana Santa

The *Semana Santa* (Holy Week) takes place in many Spanish cities during Easter week. Seville's Holy Week celebration attracts large crowds of people each year. People wearing hooded robes and others carrying large, wooden crosses walk through the streets followed by life-size statues of the Saints, the Virgin Mary, and Jesus.

This celebration began 400 years ago when the Catholic Church decided to present the story of Easter in a way that the people of Spain could understand and enjoy. In those days, many people could not read. The parade of statues showed the events of Jesus' last days to those who could not read about them in the Bible.

*A statue of the Virgin Mary is carried through the streets of Seville during the* Semana Santa *festival.*

Today, the Holy Week Festival is a celebration of faith in Christianity and the Catholic Church. Crowds fill the city streets to watch the procession of barefooted penitents who ask God to forgive their sins.

*Robed and barefoot penitents carry crosses during the Semana Santa festival in Seville.*

# Stop 3: Granada

In the foothills of the Sierra Nevada mountains, Granada sits among three hills near the Guadalquivir River in eastern Andalusia.

Granada was the last region occupied by the Moors before the Catholic rulers King Ferdinand and Queen Isabella drove them out in 1492. Many villages reveal moorish origins in their names and architecture. The name Granada itself comes from an Arabic word, *garnathah*, which means "mountain cave."

On a hilltop overlooking Granada, the Moors built a beautiful fortress 800 years ago: the *Alhambra*. Part military fort and part royal palace, the Alhambra featured schools, housing complexes, patios, and elaborate gardens, all built behind a high wall. Next to the Alhambra is the vast *Jardines del Generalif*, or "Garden of the Architect." These gardens of the Moorish kings are filled with terraces, tree-lined walks, and beautiful views of the city below.

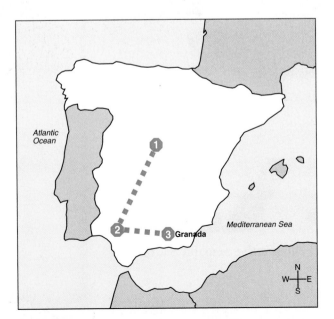

*The Alhambra fortress in Granada, with the Sierra Nevada mountains in the background.*

*Now let's fly **north** to Barcelona.*

# Growing Up in Spain

Children in Spain attend school from the ages of six to sixteen. Then, students can continue their education in vocational schools and universities, where they learn a trade, or they can begin working.

Because Spain has 17 independent regions, each with its own cultures and traditions, Spanish children sometimes speak different languages. However, most people in Spain speak Castilian Spanish, the official language. Other versions, called *dialects*, are also spoken: Catalan in Barcelona and Gallego in Galicia. The Basques of northern Spain speak an entirely different language from the rest of the country.

With so many festivals throughout the year, Spanish children learn much about their culture and history. During these festivals, children attend the *corridas* (bullfights) and watch costumed dancers perform the *flamenco* dance. Flamenco dancers wear brightly colored costumes. As they dance, they stomp their heels and clap their hands, or play castanets, rapidly in time to the music of guitars.

*Elementary schoolchildren receive instructions from their teacher.*

*Children enjoy the afternoon in the Parque Guell in Barcelona, designed by the famous Spanish architect Antoni Gaudí.*

## Stop 4: Barcelona

Barcelona sits above the steep, rocky north-eastern coast of Spain, called the *Costa Brava*, or "wild coast." Deep, blue waters stretch to the north of the city, broken up by numerous *calas* (secluded coves) and sandy, white beaches.

The *Barri Gótica* (Gothic Quarter), with its narrow, cobblestone streets and a beautiful gothic cathedral, displays more than 2,000 years of history. On Sunday afternoons, people gather in a wide plaza near the cathedral to perform a circular dance called *sardana*. This dance shows the pride that people feel for Barcelona's cultural heritage.

East of the Gothic Quarter is the modern part of the city. Here, Antoni Gaudí, a famous architect, built a strange cathedral: *Sagrada Familia* ("Holy Family"). Tall, pointed towers, curving balconies, and statues of animals and biblical characters cover the top and sides of the cathedral.

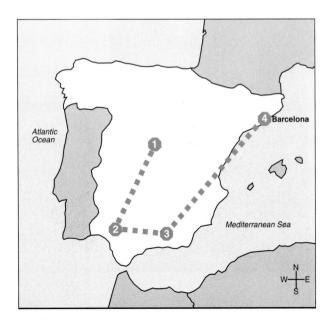

*Now let's fly **north** to the Pyrenees Mountains.*

A narrow street in the Gothic Quarter, where many famous monuments can be seen.

Below: The Plaça Reial is bordered by lampposts designed by Antoni Gaudí.

## Stop 5: Pyrenees

In the northern regions of Spain, resort cities and beaches line the Atlantic shores of Santander, while the industrial city of Burgos sits at the edge of the dry, central plains. East of Burgos is *La Rioja*, a green river valley where vineyards grow along the banks of the Ebro River.

Towering above these coastal regions and central valleys are the snowy peaks of the Pyrenees Mountains. The Pyrenees stretch for 270 miles (435 kilometers) along the Spanish-French border, forming a natural barrier between Spain and the rest of Europe. Some mountain villages have only recently built asphalt roads for cars.

The people who live in the north are proud of the traditions and folklore that distinguish them from the rest of Spain. Several versions of the Spanish language, called *dialects*, are spoken throughout this region.

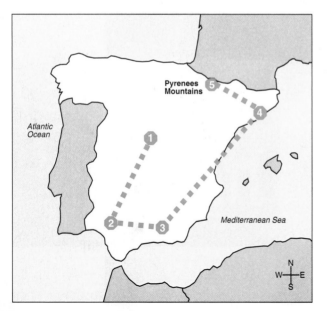

Now let's fly **west** to the Santiago de Compostela.

*Above: Sheep and goats graze in the pasture of a small village in the Pyrenees Mountains.*

*Right: The village of Viu in the Pyrenees Mountains. Until recently, many small villages like this one did not have roads for automobiles.*

# The Basque People

The Basques of northern Spain are thought to be among the first inhabitants of Spain, though exactly where they came from is a mystery. The Basque language, called *Euskera*, is also mysterious because it is not related to any other European language.

The Basques love sports, especially the national sport: *pelota vasca*, or Basqueball. This

high-speed game looks like raquetball, except players use a *cuesta* (curved basket) to catch and throw the ball. The Basques also hold strength competitions like stone lifting and log chopping.

Bilbao is an important industrial and economic center of the Basque region and the fourth largest city in Spain. The Basques value their cultural independence from the rest of Spain and the commercial success of their industrial cities. Some Basques have even fought against the central Spanish government because they want their homeland to be a separate country.

Above: Aerial view of the
Guggenheim Museum, located
in the Basque city of Bilbao.
The museum, made of limestone,
titanium, and glass, attracts
visitors from all over Europe.

Right: Basque farmer holding
a scythe, a special knife for
harvesting. The Basque people
are proud of the ancient
traditions of their culture.

## Stop 6: Santiago de Compostela

On the green hilltops and moss-covered buildings of Galicia, rain falls as frequently as it does in parts of Great Britain. In fact, the early inhabitants of Galicia, the Celts, migrated to this region from Britain.

For 900 years, Christians have traveled through the fog and heavy mists of Galicia along the *Camino de Santiago* (Way of Saint James) to visit the Cathedral of *Santiago de Compostela*. Churches and shrines fill the landscape throughout Galicia, where ancient travelers would stop for rest or food.

In 813 A.D., a hermit discovered the tomb of Saint James, an apostle of Jesus, on the western edge of Galicia called *finis terrae* ("end of the lands") by the Romans. The local Bishop built a beautiful cathedral to house the remains of Saint James, and Christians throughout Europe began to make *pilgrimages* (religious journeys) to see it.

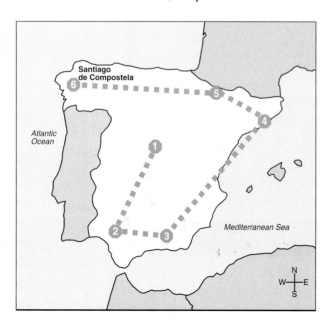

Now it's time to set sail for home.

*The cathedral of Santiago de Compostela, the final stop on the Camino de Santiago pilgrim trail, called "the way of Saint James."*

*The front entrance to the cathedral of Santiago de Compostela, where millions of travelers have ended their long pilgrimage across Europe and Spain.*

# The Foods of Spain

Spanish cooking combines sweet and spicy ingredients, an Arabic tradition that the Moors brought to Spain from North Africa. This custom continues today with the addition of sweet muscatel grapes or honeydew melon to cold soups like *gazpacho* (made with various vegetables) and *ajo blanco* (made with almonds).

Seafood is plentiful in Spain. Shrimp and prawns from the southwestern coast, as well as oysters, lobster, and crab from the northwest, are eaten by themselves or mixed with other foods like *paella.* Paella is a dish made of rice seasoned with saffron and smoked paprika.

Bars and restaurants throughout Spain serve *tapas* either with drinks or by themselves. Tapas are small portions of food, like appetizers, which usually consist of smaller versions of popular Spanish dishes. Sometimes tapas can be as simple as a bowl of stuffed olives. Tapas might also include shellfish in vinagrette sauce, fish or cured ham (called *jambon serrano*), or regional cheeses.

Spanish cooking often uses cured and roasted meats and seafood, like these Castillian dishes with cured ham, roasted chicken and lamb, and scallops.

# Glossary

**architect**     A person who designs buildings.

**calas**     Secluded coastal coves.

**corridas**     Bullfights.

**dialect**     A version of a language.

**Euskera**     The language of the Basques in northern Spain.

**flamenco**     A dance featuring colorful costumes and rhythmic music.

**mesetas**     The flat, dry plains in central Spain.

**Moors**     Muslim Arabs from North Africa who conquered Spain in the 8th century.

**mosque**     A church dedicated to *Allah*, the God of Islam.

**pelota vasca**     The Basque national sport, a lot like racquetball.

**pilgrimage**     A religious journey.

**Semana Santa**     A festival held throughout Spain during Easter.

# Further Reading

Berendes, Mary. *Spain*. Chanhassen, Minn.: Child's World, 1999.

Boast, Claire. *Spain*. Des Plaines, Ill.: Heinemann Interactive Library, 1998.

Butler, Daphne. *On the Map: Spain*. Austin, Tex.: Raintree Steck-Vaughn, 1993.

Goodwin, Bob, and Candi Perez. *A Taste of Spain*. New York: Thompson Learning, 1995.

# Suggested Web Sites

Sí Spain
<http://www.sispain.org>

All About Spain
<http://www.red2000.com>

Cyber Spain
<http://www.cyberspain.com>

# Index

**Acknowledgments and Photo Credits**
Cover: © Nik Wheeler; pp. 11, 27, 29: Tourist Office of Spain; p. 12: © PhotoDisc; pp. 12 (inset), 14, 15, 27 (inset): © Isaac Hernández/Mercury Press; pp. 17, 19, 21, 23: © 1998 Ulrike Welsch; p. 19 (below): © Nik Wheeler; pp. 24, 25: © Corbis.
Maps: Moritz Design.

| DATE | | | |
|---|---|---|---|
|  |  |  |  |
|  |  |  |  |
|  |  |  |  |
|  |  |  |  |
|  |  |  |  |
|  |  |  |  |
|  |  |  |  |
|  |  |  |  |
|  |  |  |  |
|  |  |  |  |
|  |  |  |  |
|  |  |  |  |
|  |  |  |  |